WALL PILATES WORKOUTS FOR WOMEN

Sculpt a New You in Just 30 Days! Step-by-Step Easy to Follow Illustrated Exercises to Tone Your Glutes, Strengthen Core & Achieve Perfect Posture and Balance

Alex Harper

"For the resilient women navigating life's hurdles, this book is a tribute to your strength. May it guide you on a journey of self-discovery, empowerment, and holistic well-being."

Alex Harper

Want FREE BOOKS for the rest of your LIFE?

Join our VIP club now by scanning the QR code to get FREE access to all our future books.

We ONLY send you an email when we launch a NEW BOOK. NO SPAM. Never. Ever!

Just an email with YOUR 100% OFF COUPON CODE.

CONTENTS

BEFORE YOU BEGIN

Hey, thank you for picking up this book! I have poured my heart into writing it to ensur safety and accuracy. All of the written content here has been fact-checked and cited pric to making definitive claims. The information within the pages of this book aims to guid and support women who love Pilates, and those who desire to venture into the practice

I would highly appreciate it if you left a review after reading this book. As a new autho I enjoy getting to know the transformations you have experienced through my book Your reviews will help me produce more beneficial content and motivate me to continu the work that I do. Enjoy your read!

INTRODUCTION

The Centers for Disease Control and Prevention (2022), stated that exercising can improve brain health, manage weight, improve your ability to perform daily tasks and activities, and reduce your risk of contracting diseases. In spite of all of these benefits, maintaining a consistent routine at the gym can be challenging because of our other responsibilities and mental barriers – like self-doubt – that limit us as women from achieving our fitness goals.

Wall Pilates is an effective workout that helps you transform your mind and body in the comfort of your home. No more tiring trips to the gym and feeling unmotivated. As long as you stay committed, you will achieve your fitness goals. I, too, was able to transform my body with Pilates.

My name is Alex Harper, and I am a certified fitness expert with more than a decade of experience. I know firsthand the struggles that we women face in achieving our fitness goals. From juggling work and family life to battling self-doubt, I have experienced it all. My physical transformation fueled within me a passion to create a program for women seeking efficient, results-driven workouts that can fit into their daily routine.

Picking up this book is only the start of an exciting journey for you. Within its chapters, you will find easy wall Pilates exercises that you can incorporate into your daily life. So, are you ready to get started on your journey with wall Pilates?

First, what even is wall Pilates, and how will it help you transform your mind and body? We discuss that in the next chapter.

CHAPTER 1: UNLOCKING THE POWER OF WALL PILATES

It's the mind itself which shapes the body. —Joseph Pilates

Joseph Pilates is considered the father of Pilates. He used his time in a camp during World War I to practice physical fitness. He used his fitness routines, which were influenced by various sources, such as yoga and animal movements, to aid the injured prisoners of war. He eventually perfected his Pilates practice and committed to basing his work on the principles of breath and whole-body connection, making Pilates the perfect exercise for holistic fitness. Pilates helps build an overall stronger physique; unlocking its power begins with understanding why you should practice it and knowing the many benefits it can add to your life.

Why Wall Pilates?

Did you know that engaging in unique exercise routines not only transforms the body but also triggers the release of endorphins, the body's natural mood lifters? This means that your journey to physical fitness is not just about sculpting muscles but also about nurturing your mental and emotional well-being. Wall Pilates is the same as traditional Pilates; the only difference being that the former uses a wall to add resistance to the movement, while using your body weight to create strength in your muscles.

One of Pilates's main principles is concentration. While performing Wall Pilates, it is important to maintain precision and form through gentle breathing and mental focus. The slow and controlled movements in Pilates will improve your focus and mental clarity. Although the goal of Pilates is not to make you an advanced practitioner, it is nonetheless a worthy pursuit.

With consistent practice, the meditative movements will carry over to other areas of your life and will help you become more mindful and emotionally resilient, as well as enable you to engage in your daily responsibilities with the clarity that you need to succeed.

As women, we often wear many hats and carry out various responsibilities. This can cause us to struggle with emotional and mental issues more than men, especially since we are generally perceived to be more emotional. We can turn our strong and powerful feelings into allies on our journey through life by being in sync with our bodies and minds.

Without this kind of attunement, we will continue to be controlled by our bodies' different sensations and feelings whenever we feel overwhelmed and overstimulated by day-to-day activities. Wall Pilates thus makes a great companion for women to become powerhouses by owning their minds and bodies in a powerful way.

Health Benefits of Pilates

One research conducted by the American Council on Exercise (2022) revealed that people who practiced Pilates reported feeling less stressed, which shows the profound impact this exercise can have on one's overall well-being. Pilates targets specific muscle groups to help restructure the body's shape and form, making it particularly challenging for beginners. The benefits, however, make it all worthwhile.

Improves Posture

The lengthening and stretching exercises in Pilates help reduce curvature in the spine, which leads to proper spinal alignment. The muscles that surround the spine (lower abdominal muscles, lower back muscles, and glutes) are strengthened during Pilates and are better able to support the spine, leading to improved body posture.

Improves Flexibility and Joint Health

The stretches in Pilates help improve the range of motion in your joints, which enables you to perform movements without strain, as well as your flexibility, which is your body's ability to be pulled without breaking. Increasing muscular health will enhance longevity because your risk for injuries will be lower.

Reduces Body Weight

Due to the contracting and stretching of targeted muscle groups during Pilates, you will build muscle and tone your body while reducing body fat percentage without putting too much strain on the body.

Boosts Confidence

Practicing Pilates will give you regular endorphin hits. Not only will you have a lot of energy, but you will also experience feel-good emotions that come from maintaining a good habit. Keeping commitments to yourself will always be a major booster for your self-confidence. Furthermore, the mindfulness that is practiced during Pilates can help you become more attuned to your body, making you more comfortable in it.

Overall, practicing wall Pilates will enhance your well-being, and you will feel better than you ever have. Pilates is a great form of low-impact exercise that everyone can do.

So, grab a pen, and let's get you aligned with the principles used in Pilates before you move on to try some exercises and challenges.

CHAPTER 2: PRINCIPLES OF EFFECTIVE WALL PILATES

rinciples help us understand what we are doing and why we are doing it. Without
rinciples, repeated actions can easily become meaningless, and we will become
emotivated and bored. Pilates has a set of principles that it operates on, and understanding
nem will help you reap the most benefits out of your practice. The core principles in
ilates are alignment, stability, and breathwork.

Alignment and Stability

According to the Bone Health and Osteoporosis Foundation (n.d.), alignment refers t how the spine, head, shoulders, pelvis, hips, knees, and ankles line up with each othe Improper alignment and form can lead to uncomfortable conditions like slipped dis in the lower back. Below are some simple alignment steps that you can practice whi performing Pilates to ensure that you avoid injuries and enhance your workout.

Neutral Spine

Your back has three curves: one in the neck, one in the thoracic region (middle back and one in the lower back. Maintaining a neutral spine means that all three of tho: regions are aligned. To find this alignment, lie down on your back, then bend your kne with your feet flat on the mat.

Rest your body on the mat, ensuring that you have no tension or tightness in any are then tuck your pelvis by drawing your navel toward your spine. There should be litt space between the mat and your back; if there isn't, tilt the pelvic region upwards awa from the floor.

Shoulder Position

Maintain good shoulder alignment by pulling your scapulae (shoulder blades) downwar Release any tension in your shoulders by inhaling as you lift them, then exhaling as yo gently lower them back down.

Head Alignment

Pay extra attention to your head alignment during Pilates because we normally tend keep it shrugged, bent, or however we feel like. To make sure your head is aligned wi your spine, shoulders, and pelvis, imagine an invisible line is tied to the center of you head and is pulling your head upward.

Allow this invisible line to pull your head until your neck is extended and no long curved. This shouldn't make you feel uncomfortable, but if it does, slowly drop your ey down to the floor and let your head follow until you no longer feel any discomfort tension.

Pelvic Alignment

Tuck your tailbone inward and engage your lower abdominal muscles to stabilize your pelvis. To make sure that your pelvis is in alignment with your spine, stand with your back against a wall. Next, put your hand in the space that your back makes with the wall. Then, tuck your pelvis in, lift your chest, and engage your shoulder blades–all while making sure your rib cage is expanded.

Once you've done so, check if the space between your lower back and the wall is minimal to none. That will also depend on the level of your strength and flexibility, so don't fret if you find that there is still a lot of space when you do that. As you continue practicing wall Pilates, you will get more flexible.

Hip and Knee Alignment

Your hips also have to remain in alignment with your knees. Align them by maintaining a parallel position between your hips and knees. You can also test your alignment by standing hip-width apart and avoiding bending your knees or locking them in too tightly. Don't let your knees collapse inward or push them too far outward.

Strengthening Core Stability

A strong core will help you enhance stability when practicing Pilates. It will also help improve your posture and balance. If you find it difficult to maintain body alignment and stability, focus on building strength in your core muscles. The stronger your core, the more precise your movements will be; and for us ladies who want a hotter midsection, a strong core will give you those washboard abs!

Importance of Balanced Muscle Groups

Pilates movements are centered around the core. This means that the muscles you will use to push yourself in and out of stretches are your deep abdominal and lower back muscles. Although these are the main muscle groups used, you will also need to engage your glutes, hamstrings, and inner thigh muscles to perform Pilates movements.

Thus, it is important for you to ensure that you stretch these muscles often to improve your strength. Inflexibility is not always a sign that these muscles are stiff; it can also mean that they may not be strong enough. Therefore, before and after every Pilates session, make sure you stretch these muscle groups properly.

Breathwork

Breathing is a powerful tool that we have to control our bodies. Think about it: when you breathe quickly, your heart rate also increases, and you may break into a sweat. On the other hand, when you breathe slowly, your heart rate will decrease, and your body will feel more calm.

Without being mindful of your breathing, it will be hard for you to connect with your body and honor its needs and feelings. Mindfulness will also increase your awareness of your intuition and logic, which will help you make better decisions.

Breathwork is used in Pilates to enhance the mind-body connection as you exercise so that you will be more connected to yourself and be much calmer. It likewise helps you to remain focused during the session and pay attention to your muscles and your movements. Here are a few ways you can practice breathwork during Pilates.

Core Activation Breath

The core activation breath will help you maintain stability during your Pilates session. Activate your core by inhaling deeply through your nose, making sure you fill your lower abdomen with air, and then exhaling slowly through your mouth. Repeat. If you want to feel your core activate as you practice this breathing technique, sit with your legs in a butterfly position and close your eyes as you breathe in and out.

Oxygenated Power Breath

The flow of oxygen in your body is necessary for the muscles to perform well, and a breathing technique that you can use to achieve this is lateral breathing. Deeply inhale through your nose, expanding your rib cage. Think about lifting it outwards to its left and right sides rather than upwards. Exhale gently. Repeat.

Steady Flow Breath

Steady-flow breathing is a form of relaxation technique. Adding it to your practice will help increase your concentration level. Start by inhaling through your nose as you count to four, then exhaling through your mouth as you count to four.

Then repeat slowly for a count of 10. As you keep breathing in this way, you will start to feel more relaxed and centered, helping you keep a steady tempo and come in and out of various movements smoothly during your Pilates practice.

How to Progress Week by Week

Making progress should be one of your goals in your practice. However, as women, it is easy for us to feel stressed and pressured over workout goals because of the unrealistic beauty standards that the media feeds us. Maintaining your Pilates practice as a way to get fit and get in touch with your body requires a strategy involving progressive exercises that don't put unrealistic pressure on yourself. Below are a few ways to make gentle progress in your Pilates practice.

Listening To Your Body's Signals

Pay Attention to Discomfort and Pain

Contrary to popular belief, pain and discomfort are not signs of a great workout session. Muscle soreness and pain are usually signs that you did not stretch or that you challenged yourself beyond what you were able to handle. Although it's wise to challenge yourself so that you can grow, overdoing it will actually deter your progress because you will have to pause your practice for a longer period of time to allow your muscles to heal.

Pain during your practice is also a sign that you are overworking your muscles in an unhealthy way. Pay attention to pain and discomfort, then stop to rest and check your posture and alignment to avoid injuries.

Monitor Your Breathing

Breathing is the force of life within our bodies that activates muscles and helps us shift into powerful states. Engaging in challenging movements can distract you from breathing steadily, and you may start to feel lightheaded. Always refocus on your breathing to make sure that you have enough oxygen flowing to your muscles and that you are mindful of the present moment.

Be Mindful of Fatigue and Energy Levels

During exercises, you may experience two thresholds. The first one is the mental threshold. At that stage, you will be faced with your own mental blocks and an inner critic telling you to just stop. The second threshold is your body's actual tolerance level. At that stage, you will feel fatigued, and if you push past your tolerance levels forcefully, you will get lightheaded and may injure yourself.

Pay attention to your body and your mind in order to know which threshold you are at so you can gently support yourself either by encouraging yourself to push past mental blocks or by stopping and adding another set of movements during another Pilates session.

Incorporate Progressive Intensity

Master Fundamentals

Do you remember when you had to learn math during structured education? The teachers first taught us the fundamentals of a topic, and we slowly built our ability to solve harder math problems on that foundation. Likewise, progressing in Pilates can only happen once you grasp the fundamentals of alignment, stability, and breathwork. It is from this place that more advanced movements can be built and practiced safely to achieve your goals.

Increase Repetitions

Repetitive movements help form muscle memory and your mastery of the fundamentals so that you can progress towards your goals more effectively. If you do not give yourself time to form these muscle connections through repetitions, you will compromise on form and strength.

Increasing the number of times you perform one movement also helps to sculpt and define your muscles. Repetitions also help you cross your body's physical tolerance threshold slowly, and you will find that your ability to perform more intense workouts increases over time.

Extend Duration of Holds

When you hold a position for a long period of time, you awaken your core muscles, helping you maintain stability. Because the core muscles are the powerhouse of movements, working them out will help you grow in strength and improve your posture and balance beyond the mat.

Focus on Eccentric Contractions

Eccentric movements are lengthening exercises that help to strengthen your muscles. Eccentric contractions occur when you are in a "returning" motion after engaging in a movement. The muscles are strengthened when the practitioner pays attention to the part of the body that is in motion and keeps it engaged, as opposed to losing focus and allowing the body to enter into rest.

For instance, if you do a squat, the "returning" motion would be standing back up. Instead of mindlessly standing up after squatting, keep your glutes engaged and squeeze on your way up, and just before you stand fully upright again, perform another squat.

Remaining engaged and focused during the lengthening motion of your workout wi increase your athletic ability, sculpt and define your body, and reduce injuries.

Top 3 Common Mistakes in Wall Pilates

Focusing Solely on the Core

When people think about Pilates, the first thing that comes to mind is that it is only core-building workout that tones your abs. Pilates will certainly help you develop tigh abs and a stronger core, but it will also strengthen and tone other muscle groups in you body, contributing to overall strength and flexibility.

Expecting Instant Results

A lot of celebrities who have toned bodies swear by a Pilates routine, which can mak people mistakenly believe that Pilates is a quick and easy gateway to a better body. A lc of celebrities or other fitness influencers actually have other gym routines that contribu to faster results.

Pilates will help you build your body and get you in good health, but it will happen ove time, gradually. So, if you have not yet seen the results that you desire, be patient; yo are almost there.

Ignoring Personal Limits and Pacing

As with any other exercise, it is important for you to pace yourself and listen to you body. Pushing through any pain and discomfort may result in injuries. Move at a stead pace and gradually increase the intensity of your workouts as you go along, making su that proper form and breathing are your main priorities.

Now that you have a grasp of the principles and fundamentals, it is time to get prepare with some Pilates equipment and learn how to prepare your mind and body for a Pilat session.

CHAPTER 3: PREPARATION

Your next step to starting your wall Pilates journey is to prepare what you will need to perform the exercises. Creating a space with a suitable ambience will motivate you to practice often and help increase your concentration.

Setting Up the Ideal Pilates Space

To set up an ideal space, you will first need to choose a room in your house or a particular section in one of your rooms. Make sure the space has adequate natural lighting from windows. Add some dim lights to set the tone and speakers for when you want to play some soft music.

Preparing Mentally for Each Session

Have you ever heard of the saying, "Your life goes where your mind goes?" It is true even when it comes to fitness; hence, preparing your mindset will help you get motivated to start and cultivate the discipline to create a lifestyle of fitness. These tips will direct you to a Pilates state of mind.

Remind yourself of the Benefits of Pilates

The human brain works on a reward-based system. Since the main goal of the brain is to keep us feeling safe, the brain needs to continually release feel-good hormones to the body to help communicate a sense of safety. You can hack this system to mentally motivate yourself to practice Pilates by rewarding yourself whenever you hit a significant milestone in your Pilates journey.

For example, if you find it challenging to do wall lunges, set a target for the number of repetitions before giving yourself a reward, such as a bubble bath or anything that makes you feel good. Just make sure it is something that will enhance and not hinder your health and fitness journey.

Visualize the Movements Before You Perform Them

The human brain also functions like a robot; it will start creating pathways and strategies over time to obtain whatever we input into it. For instance, when you continually talk about and think about going to the park, you will eventually feel an urge to go there.

Similarly, before your Pilates session, visualize yourself performing the wall movements; this will tell your brain to send messages to your nervous system to release emotions and energy, giving you an urge to exercise.

Remember Why You Started

Write your goals before you start practicing, and put them where you can see them. Make sure they are not vague but give a clear picture of what you would want to feel like, look like, and become over time as a result of a consistent Pilates routine. Whenever you feel unmotivated, remind yourself of your goals by reiterating them to yourself out loud.

Practice Breathwork

Breathwork helps you feel various sensations in your body without trying to avoid them or distract yourself from them. That is called emotional resilience. To overcome any tense feelings that may arise before your Pilates session, you will need emotional resilience to be consistent in your practice.

Practice deep belly breathing by inhaling for a count of four as you breathe into your lower abdomen. Hold the breath for four more counts, and then slowly exhale through your mouth. Repeat for eight more breaths.

Warm-up and Cool-down

Warming Up Effectively

To enhance your Pilates session as well as prevent injuries, you need to practice a combination of low-intensity workouts, such as marching on the spot, and dynamic stretches, such as leg swings.

Combining these two types of warm-up exercises will help your body shift into active mode, which will prevent shock to the muscles when performing more complex Pilates movements. Being in active mode also helps enhance your mind-body connection during your Pilates workout session.

Cooling Down Effectively

Cool-down movements and breathwork are designed to help your body gradually return to normal functioning at a normal heart rate. They will also help reduce muscle soreness after your Pilates session, especially if you are a beginner.

Since you will be using a lot of physical energy during your workout, it is important to cool down so that you can help the body relieve tension that may have built up while working out. As the old adage goes, "he who fails to plan ultimately fails," so remember that these preparations are essential steps to being consistent with your exercises in the long term.

Now that you have set up your space, readied your mat, and prepared your body and mind for your Pilates practice, it is time to get to the exciting part and get started with some movements.

CHAPTER 4: EXERCISES
Legs + Glutes

1. WALL SQUAT HOLDS:

Starting Position:

- Stand with your back against a wall.

- Walk your feet out in front of you, maintaining hip-width distance.

Pose 1 (Lower Position):

- Lower your body into a squat until your thighs are parallel to the ground.

Pose 2:

- Hold this static position for 20-30 seconds (or as per your comfort).

- Stand up, straightening your legs.

Tips:

Engage Core Muscles:

- Tighten your abdominal muscles to support your lower back and maintain a stable core throughout the exercise.

Optimize Depth for Intensity:

- To increase the challenge, gradually sink lower into the squat position over time.

2

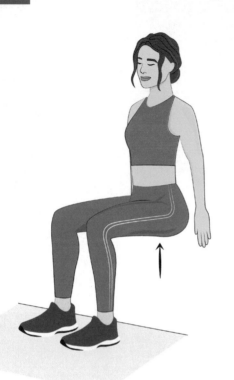

Starting Position:

- Stand with your back against a wall.
- Lower your body into a squat position, ensuring your back is against the wall, and your knees are directly above your ankles.

Pose 1 (Lower Squat):

- Slide your body down the wall, bending your knees into a lower squat position.

Pose 2 (Higher Squat):

- Push through your legs to rise up, returning to the semi squat position.
- Repeat the sliding movement for 10 - 15 repetitions, alternating between lower and higher squat positions.

Tips:

Controlled Sliding:

- Emphasize controlled, deliberate sliding motions to maximize muscle engagement and maintain balance.

Adjust Squat Depth:

- Vary the intensity by adjusting the depth of your squat. Lowering deeper engages muscles more intensely while rising higher adds variety to the exercise.

3. WALL LATERAL SQUATS:

Starting Position:
- Stand facing the wall with your feet wider than shoulder-width apart.
- Place your hands on the wall for support, keeping your back straight and chest lifted.

Pose 1 (Squatting to the Side):
- Shift your weight to one side, bending the knee while keeping the opposite leg straight.
- Lower into a lateral squat position, ensuring the bent knee aligns with your toes.

Pose 2 (Returning to Center):
- Push through the bent leg to return to the starting position.
- Perform 10-15 repetitions on one side before switching.

Tips:

Hip Flexibility:
- Focus on gradually increasing your hip flexibility to achieve a deeper lateral squat over time.

Steady Hand Placement:
- Maintain steady hand placement on the wall for support, allowing you to concentrate on the squatting movement.

4. WALL SIDEKICKS:

Starting Position:

- Stand facing the wall with both hands resting on it for support.
- Place your feet together or hip-width apart, depending on your comfort.

Pose 1 (Kicking Outward):

- Kick one leg to the side, keeping it straight or slightly bent.
- Extend the leg outward, reaching towards your maximum range of motion.

Pose 2 (Returning):

- Bring the leg back to the starting position.
- Perform 10-15 repetitions for each leg, kicking the leg outward in a dynamic motion.

Tip:

Controlled Movement:

- Execute controlled kicks to focus on muscle engagement and avoid swinging the leg with momentum.

5. WALL KICKBACKS:

5

Starting Position:
- Stand facing the wall with your hands placed on it for support, shoulder-width apart.
- Position your feet hip-width apart and ensure your back is straight.

Pose 1 (Kickback):
- Lift one leg straight behind you, engaging your glutes and hamstring muscles.
- Extend the leg as far back as comfortable, feeling a contraction in your glutes.
- Hold the extended contracted position for 1-2 seconds.

Pose 2 (Returning):
- Bring the leg back to the starting position, keeping movements controlled.
- Perform 10-15 repetitions, kicking the leg backward in a dynamic motion.

Tip:

Controlled Range of Motion:
- Focus on controlled kickbacks, avoiding excessive swinging, to target the glutes and hamstrings effectively.

6

Starting Position:

- Start facing the wall in an all-fours position with your hands placed firmly on the floor shoulder-width apart.

- Keep your wrists aligned under your shoulders and your knees under your hips.

Pose 1 (Kicking Upward):

- Lift your right leg towards the ceiling and squeeze your glutes at the top.

- Place your left hand on the wall for additional abdominal engagement.

Pose 2 (Lowering Leg):

- Lower the leg back down to starting position.

- Perform 10-15 repetitions on one leg before switching your legs and hands.

Tips:

Squeeze Glutes at the Top:

- Emphasize squeezing your glutes a the top of the kick to fully engage an activate the muscles.

Controlled Movement:

- Execute each donkey kick with contro focusing on deliberate and controlle movements rather than relying o momentum.

7. WALL LUNGES:

7

Starting Position:

- Stand facing from the wall with your hands on your hips.

- Position one foot in front of you and the other with the lifted heel against the wall.

- Ensure your front knee is directly above the ankle.

Pose 1 (Lunging):

- Lower your body into a lunge position, bending your front knee to about a 90-degree angle.

- Hold the lunge position for 1-2 seconds for a static contraction (optional)

Pose 2 (Returning):

- Push through the front heel to return to the starting position.

- Perform 10 repetitions for each leg

Tip:

Controlled Movements:

- Execute lunges with controlled movements, emphasizing muscle engagement and avoiding rapid or unsteady motions.

8

8. WALL HIP THRUSTS:

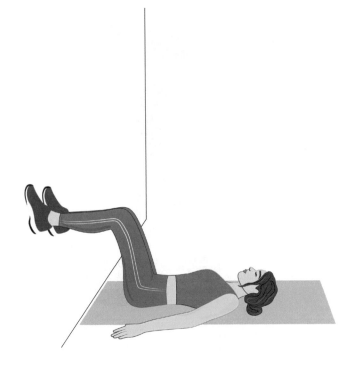

Starting Position:

- Lie on your back with your feet flat against a wall and your knees bent at a 90-degree angle.

- Place your arms by your sides, palms facing down for stability.

- Ensure your feet are hip-width apart and your back is flat on the floor.

Pose 1 (Hip Thrust):

- Press through your heels, lifting your hips towards the ceiling.

- Squeeze your glutes at the top and hold for 1-2 seconds.

Pose 2 (Lowering):

- Lower your hips back down, maintaining a slight hover above the floor.

- Perform 10 -15 repetitions, maintaining a controlled pace.

Tips:

Full Hip Extension:

- Focus on achieving a full hip extension at the top to engage the glutes more effectively.

Heel Pressure on Wall:

- Keep consistent pressure on your heels against the wall.

9. WALL PIKE LEG EXTENSIONS:

Starting Position:

- Begin in a push-up position with your hands on the floor shoulder-width apart and your feet against the wall.

Pose 1 (Bending Legs):

- Bend and hover your knees close to the ground for a moment.

Pose 2 (Leg Extension):

- Extend your legs back towards the wall, lifting your hips towards the ceiling.

Tip:

Smooth Transitions:

- Emphasize smooth transitions between bending and extending your legs, avoiding sudden movements for better control.

10

10. WALL CALF RAISES:

Starting Position:

- Stand facing a wall with your hands resting on it for support.
- Place your feet hip-width apart, with heels flat on the ground.
- Keep your knees straight throughout the exercise for optimal engagement.

Pose 1 (Raising Heels):

- Lift your heels off the ground, rising onto the balls of your feet.

Pose 2 (Lowering Heels):

- Slowly lower your heels back down towards the floor, feeling a stretch in your calf muscles.
- Perform 10-15 repetitions, maintaining a controlled pace.

Tips:

Full Range of Motion:

- Aim for a full range of motion, lifting your heels as high as comfortable and lowering them to feel a stretch in your calves.

Progressive Intensity:

- Gradually increase the intensity by changing the distance of your feet from the wall or trying single-leg calf raises

Core Exercises

11. WALL PLANK:

11

Starting Position:

- Stand facing the wall, approximately an arm's length away.

- Place your hands on the wall at shoulder height, fingers pointing upward.

- Walk your feet back and stand on your toes (heels elevated), keeping them hip-width apart, until your body forms a straight line.

Pose 1 (Plank Position):

- Engage your core, glutes, and legs as you lean forward, creating a plank position against the wall.

- Ensure your arms are straight, and your shoulders are directly above your wrists.

Pose 2 (Hold):

- Hold the plank position for 20-30 seconds

- Focus on a strong and stable core.

Tip:

Challenge Yourself:

- To intensify the plank, lift one foot a few inches off the ground.

12

12. WALL SIDE PLANK:

Starting Position:

- Stand with your side facing the wall, about an arm's length away.
- Place your forearm against the wall, elbow directly below your shoulder.
- Keep your feet together or staggered for stability.

Pose 1 (Side Plank Lift):

- Lift your hips, creating a straight line from your head to your heels.
- Engage your core and keep your body in a sideways position.

Pose 2 (Hold):

- Hold the side plank position, ensuring your body remains aligned for 20 - 30 seconds for each side.
- Keep your shoulder, hip, and ankle stacked vertically.

Tips:

Engage Core and Glutes:

- Squeeze your core and glutes to maintain a stable and straight body position.

Maintain Shoulder Alignment:

- Ensure your shoulder is directly above your elbow to prevent unnecessary strain.

Challenge Yourself:

- Keep the top leg lifted for an extra challenge.

13

13. WALL TOE TOUCHES:

Starting Position:

- Lie on your back with your legs extended up the wall.
- Reach your arms straight up toward the ceiling, perpendicular to the floor.
- Keep your lower back pressed into the ground.

Pose 1 (Toe Touch):

- Engage your abdominal muscles as you lift your upper body off the ground, reaching your fingertips toward your toes.
- Aim to touch your toes or get as close as comfortably possible.

Pose 2 (Returning):

- Lower your upper body back to the ground
- Repeat the movement for 10 repetitions.

Tip:

Intensify Abdominal Engagement:

- Lift your shoulder blades off the ground and visualize bringing your ribcage closer to your pelvis for a more intense abdominal contraction.

14

14. WALL ABDOMINAL CRUNCHES:

Starting Position:

- Lie on your back with your legs extended up the wall.

- Place your hands behind your head, elbows pointing out to the sides.

- Keep your lower back pressed into the ground.

Pose 1 (Crunch):

- Engage your abdominal muscles as you lift your upper body off the ground, bringing your shoulder blades towards your knees.

- Keep your lower back on the ground.

Pose 2 (Lowering Down):

- Lower your upper body back to the ground with control, allowing your shoulder blades to lightly touch the ground.

- Repeat the movement for 10 repetitions

Tips:

Increase Difficulty:

- To intensify the crunch, hold the contracted position for a moment.

Controlled Movements:

- Perform the crunches with controlled movements, ensuring a smooth upward motion and controlled lowering.

15. WALL MOUNTAIN CLIMBERS:

15

Starting Position:

- Stand facing the wall with your palms pressed against it, arms extended.
- Place your hands at shoulder height, slightly wider than shoulder-width apart.
- Step back a bit, allowing your body to angle away from the wall, keeping your feet hip-width apart.

Pose 1 (Knee Drive):

- Drive one knee towards your chest, engaging your core and maintaining a strong upper body position against the wall.
- Keep your shoulders higher than your wrists.

Pose 2 (Switching Legs):

- Quickly switch legs, bringing the other knee towards your chest while extending the first leg back.
- Continue to alternate legs in a dynamic, rhythmic motion for 15-20 reps.

Tip:

Elevate Intensity:

- Increase the challenge by performing the mountain climbers at a faster pace, intensifying the cardiovascular and core workout.

16

16. WALL TOUCHES:

Starting Position:

- Start with a push-up position facing the wall, with your hands on the floor.

Pose 1 (Touching Wall):

- Lift one hand off the floor and reach towards the wall, tapping it with your fingertips.

- Maintain a stable and engaged core to prevent excessive hip movement.

Pose 2 (Switching Hands):

- Return the touched hand to the floor while lifting the other hand to touch the wall.

- Continue alternating between hands for 3 -5 repetitions for each hand.

Tip:

Controlled Movements:

- Execute the touches with controlled movements, focusing on stability and precision to maintain proper form.

17

17. ABDOMINAL TWISTS:

Starting Position:

- Sit on the floor with your knees bent, feet flat on the ground, and your back at a slight reclined angle.

- Lift your feet and place them on the wall, creating a semi-crunch position with your torso leaning back.

- Keep your hands together.

Pose 1 (Twist):

- Rotate your torso and shoulders to one side, bringing your elbow towards the ground.

- Aim to touch the ground beside your hip.

Pose 2 (Return):

- Rotate back to the center, maintaining control throughout the movement.

- Repeat the twist to the other side, alternating between sides for 10 reps per side.

Tips:

Engage Core Muscles:

- Keep your core muscles engaged to stabilize your spine and enhance the effectiveness.

Full Range of Motion:

- Rotate as far as comfortable, striving for a full range of motion.

18

18. WALL SCISSORS KICKS:

Starting Position:

- Lie on your back with your hips close to the wall.

- Place your hands under your hips for support and extend your legs up against the wall.

- Keep your legs straight with a slight bend in the knees.

Pose 1 (V Shape - Leg Slide):

- Slide both legs down the wall, creating a V shape by smoothly opening them to the sides.

- Feel the stretch along your inner thighs and maintain control throughout the sliding movement.

Pose 2 (Returning - Core Engagement)

- Engage your core as you bring both legs back up to the starting position sliding them along the wall.

Tip:

Controlled V Shape:

- Slide your legs smoothly, creating a V shape, and focus on the stretch and contraction of your inner thighs.

19

19. WALL DEAD BUG:

Starting Position:

- Lie on your back with your head close to the wall.

- Place your hands against the wall.

- Bend your knees at a 90-degree angle and lift your feet, so your shins are parallel to the ground.

Pose 1 (Leg Extension):

- While keeping your hands on the wall, straighten one leg, reaching preferably without touching the ground.

- Simultaneously, maintain the opposite leg in the starting position, and keep your lower back pressed into the ground.

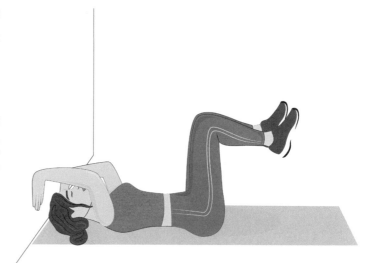

Pose 2 (Returning - Controlled Bend):

- Engage your core as you bend the extended leg and return it to the starting position.

- Repeat the movement with the other leg, alternating between legs. Aim for 5 -10 repetitions per each leg.

Tip:

Controlled Movements:

- Perform the leg extension with control, avoiding any sudden or jerky motions.

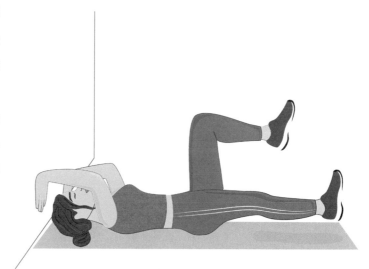

Arms + Shoulders

20

20. WALL PUSH-UPS:

Starting Position:

- Stand facing the wall with your fee[t] shoulder-width apart.

- Place your hands on the wall slight[ly] below shoulder height and a little wid[er] than shoulder-width apart.

- Step back to create a comfortabl[e] distance between you and the wall.

Pose 1 (Lowering Chest):

- Bend your elbows and lower you[r] chest towards the wall, keeping you[r] body in a straight line.

- Ensure your elbows are at a 90-degr[ee] angle.

Pose 2 (Pushing Back Up):

- Push through your palms to retur[n] to the starting position, straightenin[g] your arms.

- Perform 15-20 repetitions.

Tips:

Adjust Distance for Intensity:

- Modify the difficulty by adjustin[g] your distance from the wall. Th[e] closer you are, the easier it is; th[e] farther you are, the more challengin[g] the exercise becomes.

21. DIAMOND WALL PUSH-UPS:

21

Starting Position:

- Stand facing the wall with your feet hip-width apart.
- Place your hands on the wall, forming a diamond shape with your thumbs and index fingers.
- Keep your arms straight and your body in a plank position.

Pose 1 (Lowering Chest):

- Bend your elbows, lowering your chest towards the wall while maintaining the diamond shape.
- Ensure your body forms a straight line.

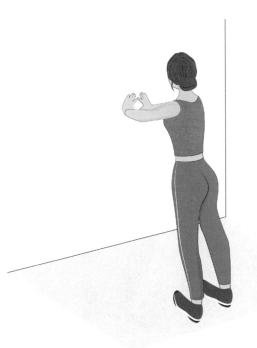

Pose 2 (Pushing Back Up):

- Push through your palms to return to the starting position, straightening your arms.
- Perform 10-15 repetitions.

Tip:

Focus on Triceps and Chest:

- Emphasize the engagement of your triceps and chest muscles during each push-up, maximizing the benefits.

22

22. WALL TRICEPS EXTENSIONS:

Starting Position:

- Stand facing the wall, about an arm's length away.
- Place your hands on the wall at shoulder height, shoulder-width apart.
- Step back, leaning your body forward, and keep your feet hip-width apart.

Pose 1 (Bending Elbows):

- Bend your elbows, bringing your forehead towards the wall, keeping your hands close to your head. Forearms are now on the wall.
- Ensure a 90-degree angle at your elbows.

Pose 2 (Straightening Arms):

- Push through your palms to straighten your arms, returning to the starting position.
- Perform 12-15 repetitions.

Tips:

Focus on Triceps Engagement:

- Emphasize the contraction of you triceps during the extension by full straightening your arms.

Stable Core:

- Engage your core muscles to maintai stability and prevent excessive archin or sagging of the lower back.

23. WALL ARM CIRCLES:

Starting Position:

- Stand sideways close to the wall, with your feet shoulder-width apart.

- Raise your arm in front of you. Place the back of your hand on the wall at shoulder height, fingers pointing forward.

- Keep your arm straight, and your body in a neutral position.

Pose 1 (Forward Arm Circles):

- Begin making a circle with your hand touching the wall, moving backward.

Pose 2 (Reverse Arm Circles):

- Change the direction of the circles, moving your arm forward. Keep constant contact between your hand and the wall.

- Continue the motion for 5-10 circles before switching your hands.

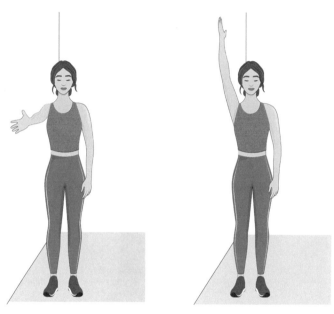

Tips:

Focus on Shoulder Mobility:

- Emphasize the mobility of your shoulder by maintaining a smooth and controlled circular motion.

Wall for Stability:

- Utilize the wall for stability, allowing you to focus on the quality of the arm circles without worrying about balance.

24

24. MOVE THE WALL:

Starting Position:

- Stand facing the wall with your feet hip-width apart.

- Place your hands on the wall at shoulder height.

- Keep your arms straight, and your core engaged.

Pose 1 (Pressing into the Wall):

- Press your hands firmly into the wall, engaging your chest and shoulder muscles.

- Hold the pressed position for 20-30 seconds for an isometric contraction.

Pose 2 (Relaxing):

- Release the pressure on the wall and relax your arms.

- Repeat the isometric press for 1-3 sets (optional).

Tip:

Maintain Consistent Pressure:

- Keep a consistent and controlled pressure on the wall throughout the isometric press for optimal muscle engagement.

25. WALL LATERAL PULLDOWN:

25

Starting Position:

- Stand with your back against the wall, ensuring good posture.

- Extend your arms overhead, touching the wall with your arms slightly wider than shoulder-width apart.

Pose 1 (Pulling Down):

- Pull your arms down and towards the sides, bringing your elbows towards your waist.

- Squeeze your shoulder blades together, engaging the upper back muscles.

Pose 2 (Returning):

- Slowly release the tension, allowing your arms to return to the overhead position.

- Perform 10-15 repetitions.

Tips:

Maintain Back Against Wall:

- Ensure your back stays in contact with the wall throughout the exercise to maximize stability and isolate the targeted muscles.

Focus on Shoulder Blade Squeeze:

- Emphasize the squeeze of your shoulder blades during the pulldown to activate and strengthen the upper back.

26

26. WALL SUPPORTED SIDE PLANK WITH ARM RAISES:

Starting Position:

- Stand with your side facing the wall, about an arm's length away.

- Place your bottom elbow close to the wall and press your forearm against it for support.

- Lift your hips, forming a straight line from your head to your feet.

Pose 1 (Arm Raise):

- While maintaining the side plank position, lift your top arm towards the ceiling.

- Hold the raised position for 1 second.

Pose 2 (Lowering Arm):

- Lower your arm back down to the starting position.

- Perform 15 - 20 arm raises on one side before switching.

Tip:

Stable Hips:

- Focus on keeping your hips stable and preventing them from dropping during the arm raises to engage your obliques effectively.

27. WALL SEATED ARM PULSES:

Starting Position:

- Sit on the floor with your back against the wall.

- Extend your legs in front of you and keep them hip-width apart.

Pose 1 (Lateral Pulses):

- Lift your arms slightly to the sides, palms facing down

- Perform small, controlled pulses up and down, targeting the lateral shoulder muscles.

- Continue the lateral pulsing motion for 10-20 seconds.

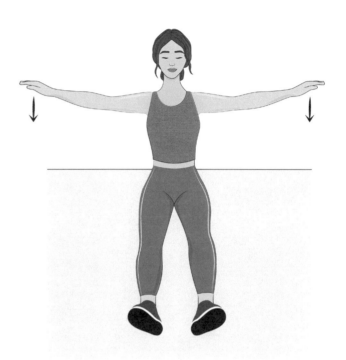

Tips:

Focus on Lateral Delts:

- Emphasize the lateral deltoids by directing the pulsing motion outward.

Maintain Back Against Wall:

- Keep your back against the wall to stabilize your posture and isolate the lateral shoulder muscles.

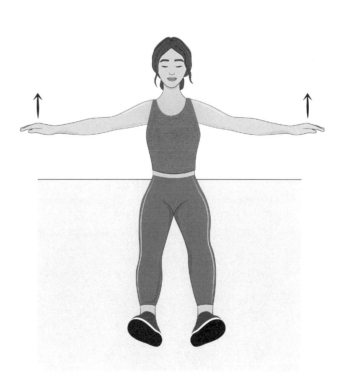

28. SEATED SIDE BENDS:

Starting Position:

- Sit on the floor with your back against the wall.

- Extend your legs in front of you, keeping them hip-width apart.

- Hands are resting on your thighs.

Pose 1 (Side Bending):

- Inhale and lift one arm overhead, reaching towards the opposite side, creating a lateral stretch along your torso.

- Feel the stretch along your side as you bend gently.

Pose 2 (Returning):

- Exhale and return to the starting position.

- Repeat on the other side, alternating between left and right for 10 repetitions.

Tip:

Lengthen Through the Side:

- Focus on lengthening your side as you perform the side bends, creating a stretch along the torso.

Posture

29. WALL CHEST OPENER:

Starting Position:

- Stand sideways next to the wall with your feet hip-width apart.
- Extend your arm behind your body while placing your palm on the wall at shoulder height.

Pose 1 (Chest Opening):

- Slowly rotate your torso away from the wall, allowing your chest to open up.
- Feel the stretch across the front of your chest and shoulder. Hold for at least 5 -10 seconds

Pose 2 (Returning):

- Gently rotate your torso back to the starting position.
- Switch sides

Tips:

Focus on Pectoral Stretch:

- Emphasize the stretch in your chest muscles as you rotate away from the wall.

Steady Breathing:

- Maintain a steady breathing rhythm to enhance relaxation and flexibility during the chest opener.

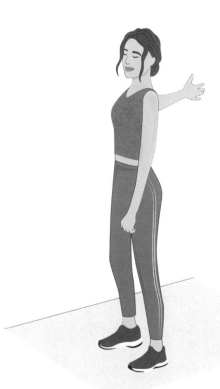

30

30. WALL THORACIC ELBOW EXTENSION:

Starting Position:

- Stand facing the wall with your elbows pressed against the wall.

- Place your hands together behind your head, keeping your elbows on the wall and pointing forward.

- Your hands should be around the neck area.

Pose 1 (Elbow Extension):

- Slowly lift your elbows upward, allowing your chest to move closer to the wall.

- Feel the extension in your thoracic spine and a stretch in your chest and upper back for 10 seconds.

Pose 2 (Returning):

- Gently lower your elbows back to the starting position, maintaining a controlled movement.

- Repeat the extension 1-3 times

Tips:

Maintain Hands Behind Head:

- Keep your hands together behind your head throughout the movement ensuring a consistent stretch.

31. WALL DOWNWARD FACING DOG:

Starting Position:

- Stand facing the wall, about an arm's length away.
- Place your hands on the wall at shoulder height, fingers pointing upward.
- Walk your feet back, hip-width apart.

Pose 1 (Downward Dog):

- Push your hands forward into the wall as you pull your hips away from the wall.

Pose 2 (Hold):

- Hold the downward dog position, lengthening through your spine and stretching your hamstrings and calves.
- Breathe deeply and relax your neck, allowing your head to hang naturally. Hold for 20 seconds.

Tips:

Heels Toward Floor:

- Aim to bring your heels as close to the floor as comfortable, feeling a stretch in your calves and hamstrings.

Relax Neck and Shoulders:

- Let your head hang freely, allowing your neck and shoulders to relax, promoting a gentle stretch.

32

32. CHIN TUCKS AGAINST WALL:

Starting Position:

- Stand with your back against the wall, ensuring your feet are hip-width apart.

- Keep your head, upper back, and buttocks in contact with the wall.

- Relax your shoulders and let your arms hang naturally by your sides.

Pose 1 (Chin Tuck):

- Gently draw your chin toward your chest, creating a subtle tucking motion without lifting your head off the wall.

- Focus on lengthening the back of your neck.

Pose 2 (Hold):

- Hold the chin-tucked position for a few 15 seconds, feeling a stretch along the back of your neck and upper spine. Return to the starting position. Repeat 1-3 times.

Tips:

Gentle Neck Stretch:

- Aim for a comfortable stretch rather than forcing your chin too close to your chest.

Maintain Upper Back Contact:

- Keep the upper back in contact with the wall throughout the movement to isolate the neck muscles.

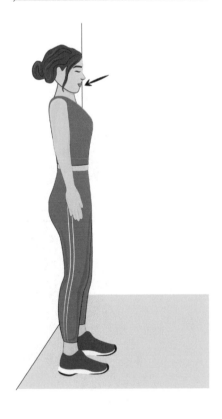

33. WALL ROLL DOWN:

Starting Position:

- Stand with your back against the wall, ensuring your feet are hip-width apart.
- Keep a slight bend in your knees and relax your shoulders.

Pose 1 (Forward Bend):

- Inhale as you start to tuck your chin to your chest and slowly articulate your spine down, bringing your torso toward the ground.

Pose 2 (Roll Down):

- Exhale and continue rolling down, segment by segment, until your hands reach the floor or a comfortable range.
- Keep your knees slightly bent and relax your neck.

Tips:

Segmented Movement:

- Roll down through each vertebra, creating a sequential movement to promote flexibility in the spine.

Maintain Connection:

- Keep your legs connected to the wall as much as possible during the descent.

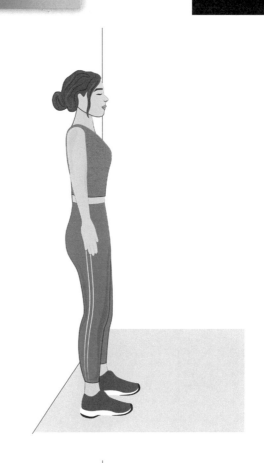

Flexibility & Balance

34. WALL FOREARM STRETCH:

Starting Position:

- Stand facing the wall with your feet hip-width apart.

- Extend your arm straight in front of you and place the palm against the wall at shoulder height.

Pose 1 (Arm Stretch):

- Press your palm against the wall, fingers pointing downward.

- Hold the stretch for about 20 seconds.

Tips:

Gentle Pressure:

- Apply a gentle and controlled pressure against the wall to avoid overstretching.

Breathe and Relax:

- Breathe deeply and relax into the stretch, allowing the tension in your forearm to gradually release.

35

35. WALL ASSISTED SIDE LUNGE STRETCH:

Starting Position:

- Stand facing the wall with your feet wider than shoulder-width apart.
- Place your hands on the wall at shoulder height for support.
- Keep your toes pointed forward.

Pose 1 (Side Lunge):

- Shift your body weight to one side, bending the knee of the lunging leg while keeping the other leg straight.

Pose 2 (Stretch):

- Hold the side lunge position, feeling the stretch along the inner thigh of the lunging leg.
- After holding the stretch, return to the starting position and switch to the other leg, alternating between sides for 15 seconds per one side.

Tips:

Controlled Movement:

- Lower into the side lunge with control, focusing on the stretch along the inner thigh.

Knee alignment:

- Ensure your knee is aligned with your toes and your opposite leg is straight.

36

36. WALL SUPPORTED SINGLE SQUAT:

Starting Position:

- Stand facing the wall with your feet about hip-width apart.
- Place your hands on the wall at shoulder height for support.
- Keep your back straight, shoulders relaxed, and core engaged.

Pose 1 (Single Leg Lift):

- Lift one foot off the ground, bend the knee and lift the heel towards your glutes.
- Keep the other foot firmly on the ground.

Pose 2 (Squat):

- Lower your body into a partial squat position on the standing leg, keeping your back straight and chest up.
- Perform 5 -10 repetitions for each leg.

Tip:

Controlled Movement:

- Lower into the squat with control keeping your movements smooth and controlled.

37. WALL SINGLE LEG BALANCE:

Starting Position:

- Stand with your back against the wall and lower your body into a sitting position, forming a more than 90-degree angle at your knees (semi squat).

- Place your hands on your hips or keep them relaxed by your sides.

Pose 1 (Wall Sit):

- Engage your core and keep your weight on your heels.

Pose 2 (Single Leg Lift):

- Lift one leg off the ground, extending it straight in front of you.

- Hold the position for 10-15 seconds maintaining the wall sit with the opposite leg lifted. Switch legs.

Tip:

Adjustable Squat Depth:

- For added difficulty, aim for a 90-degree angle at the knees during the wall sit, intensifying the engagement of your leg muscles.

38

38. PLANTAR FASCIA STRETCH:

Starting Position:

- Stand facing a wall with your hands resting against it for support.
- Lift one foot and place your toes against the wall, keeping the heel on the ground.
- Ensure the foot is flexed, pointing the toes upward.

Pose 1 (Setup):

- Position your toes against the wall, creating a stretch along the bottom of your foot.
- Keep your knee straight and aligned with your hip.

Pose 2 (Stretch):

- Gently lean your body forward, maintaining the toes against the wall.
- Feel the stretch along the plantar fascia and the underside of your foot.

Tip:

Hold and Breathe:

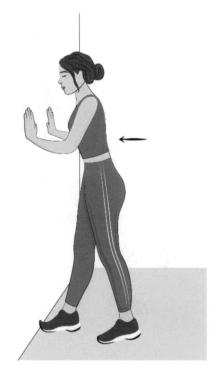

- Hold the stretch for 15 seconds, breathing deeply and allowing the tension in the plantar fascia to release.

39

39. WALL QUAD STRETCH:

Starting Position:

- Stand facing a wall with your hands resting against it for support.

Pose 1 (Setup):

- Lift your heel towards your buttocks, feeling a stretch in the front of the thigh (quadriceps) of the lifted leg.

- Keep your knees close together.

Pose 2 (Stretch):

- Gently pull your ankle towards your buttocks, increasing the stretch in the quadriceps.

- After holding the stretch for about 10 seconds, switch to the other leg to ensure both quadriceps receive attention.

Tip:

Enhancing the Stretch:

- To intensify the stretch, consider moving slightly further from the wall and, while maintaining balance, tilt your upper body forward. You should feel increased tension in your quad.

40

40. "FIGURE 4" WALL HIP STRETCH:

Starting Position:

- Lie on your back with your legs facing the wall.

- Bend your knees (90-degrees) and place your feet flat on the wall, hip-width apart.

- Keep your lower back pressed into the ground.

Pose 1 (Setup):

- Lift your right leg and place your right ankle on top of your left knee, creating a "figure 4" shape.

Pose 2 (Stretch):

- Push with your right hand into your right knee to maximize the stretch in your right hip and glute.

- Hold the position for about 10 seconds

- Switch to the other leg and repeat the stretch.

Tip:

Hip Position:

- Experiment with the angle of you bent knee to find the most comfortabl and effective position for your hip.

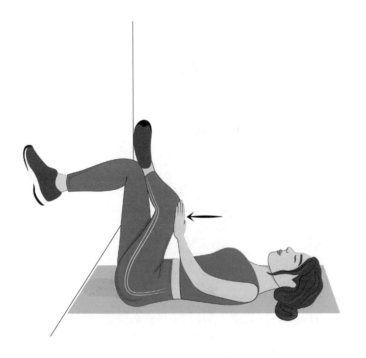

CHAPTER 5: 30-DAY CHALLENGE

Day 1

Exercise	Number	Reps / Duration
Wall Quad Stretch	39	15 Seconds
Wall Squats Holds	1	20-30 Seconds
Wall Plank	11	20-30 Seconds
Wall Push-Ups	20	15 - 20 Reps
Wall Sidekicks	4	10 - 15 Reps
Wall Toe Touches	13	10 Reps
Wall Chest Opener	29	15 Seconds

Day 2

Exercise	Number	Reps / Duration
Plantar Fascia Stretch	38	15 Seconds
Wall Squad Sliding	2	10 Reps
Wall Side Plank	12	20-30 Seconds
Wall Arm Circles	23	5-10 Reps
Wall Kickbacks	5	10 - 15 Reps
Wall Abdominal Crunches	14	10 Reps
Wall Thoracic Elbow Extension	30	2 X 10 Seconds

Day 3

Exercise	Number	Reps / Duration
Wall Assisted Side Lunge Stretch	35	15 Seconds / Side
Wall Lateral Squad	3	10 - 15 Reps
Abdominal Twist	17	20 Reps
Diamond Wall Pushups	21	10 - 15 Reps
Wall Donkey Kicks	6	10-15 Reps
Wall Mountain Climber	15	15 - 20 Reps
Wall Downward Facing Dog	31	20 Seconds

Day 4

Exercise	Number	Reps / Duration
Forearm Stretch	34	20 Seconds
Wall Lunges	7	10 Reps
Wall Touches	16	10 Reps
Move the Wall	22	20-30 Seconds
Wall Hip Thrust	8	10 - 15 Reps
Wall Scissors Kicks	18	15 - 20 Reps
Chin Tucks Against Wall	32	15 Seconds

Day 5

Exercise	Number	Reps / Duration
Wall Single Leg Balance	37	10 - 15 Seconds
Wall Kickbacks	5	10 - 15 Reps
Wall Dead Bug	19	5 - 10 Reps
Move the Wall	24	20-30 Seconds
Wall Pike Leg Extension	9	10 Reps
Wall Mountain Climbers	15	15 - 20 Reps
Wall Roll Down	33	20 Seconds

Day 6

Exercise	Number	Reps / Duration
Wall Supported Single Squat	36	5 -10 Reps
Wall Hip Thrust	8	10 - 15 Reps
Wall Touches	16	10 Reps
Wall Lateral Pulldown	25	10 - 15 Reps
Wall Calf Raises	10	10 - 15 Reps
Seated Side Bends	28	10 Reps
Wall Downward Facing Dog	31	20 Seconds

Day 7

Exercise	Number	Reps / Duration
Wall Quad Stretch	39	15 Seconds
Wall Squats Holds	1	20-30 Seconds
Wall Plank	11	20-30 Seconds
Wall Push-Ups	20	15 - 20 Reps
Wall Sidekicks	4	10 - 15 Reps
Wall Toe Touches	13	10 Reps
Wall Chest Opener	29	15 Seconds

Day 8

Exercise	Number	Reps / Duration
Plantar Fascia Stretch	38	15 Seconds
Wall Squad Sliding	2	10 Reps
Wall Side Plank	12	20-30 Seconds
Wall Arm Circles	23	5-10 Reps
Wall Kickbacks	5	10 - 15 Reps
Wall Abdominal Crunches	14	10 Reps
Wall Thoracic Elbow Extension	30	2 X 10 Seconds

Day 9

Exercise	Number	Reps / Duration
Wall Assisted Side Lunge Stretch	35	15 Seconds / Side
Wall Lateral Squad	3	10 - 15 Reps
Abdominal Twist	17	20 Reps
Diamond Wall Pushups	21	10 - 15 Reps
Wall Donkey Kicks	6	10-15 Reps
Wall Mountain Climber	15	15 - 20 Reps
Wall Downward Facing Dog	31	20 Seconds

Day 10

Exercise	Number	Reps / Duration
Forearm Stretch	34	20 Seconds
Wall Lunges	7	10 Reps
Wall Touches	16	10 Reps
Move the Wall	22	20-30 Seconds
Wall Hip Thrust	8	10 - 15 Reps
Wall Scissors Kicks	18	15 - 20 Reps
Chin Tucks Against Wall	32	15 Seconds

Day 11

Exercise	Number	Reps / Duration
Wall Single Leg Balance	37	10 - 15 Seconds
Wall Kickbacks	5	10 - 15 Reps
Wall Dead Bug	19	5 - 10 Reps
Move the Wall	24	20-30 Seconds
Wall Pike Leg Extension	9	10 Reps
Wall Mountain Climber	15	15 - 20 Reps
Wall Roll Down	33	20 Seconds

Day 12

Exercise	Number	Reps / Duration
Wall Supported Single Squat	36	5 -10 Reps
Wall Hip Thrust	8	10 - 15 Reps
Wall Touches	16	10 Reps
Wall Side Plank with Arm Raises	25	10 - 15 Reps
Wall Calf Raises	10	10 - 15 Reps
Seated Side Bends	28	10 Reps
Wall Downward Facing Dog	31	20 Seconds

Day 13

Exercise	Number	Reps / Duration
Wall Quad Stretch	39	15 Seconds
Wall Squats Holds	1	20-30 Seconds
Wall Plank	11	20-30 Seconds
Wall Push-Ups	20	15 - 20 Reps
Wall Sidekicks	4	10 - 15 Reps
Wall Toe Touches	13	10 Reps
Wall Chest Opener	29	15 Seconds

Day 14

Exercise	Number	Reps / Duration
Plantar Fascia Stretch	38	15 Seconds
Wall Squad Sliding	2	10 Reps
Wall Side Plank	12	20-30 Seconds
Wall Arm Circles	23	5-10 Reps
Wall Kickbacks	5	10 - 15 Reps
Wall Abdominal Crunches	14	10 Reps
Wall Thoracic Elbow Extension	30	2 X 10 Seconds

Day 15

Exercise	Number	Reps / Duration
Wall Assisted Side Lunge Stretch	35	15 Seconds / Side
Wall Lateral Squad	3	10 - 15 Reps
Abdominal Twist	17	20 Reps
Diamond Wall Pushups	21	10 - 15 Reps
Wall Donkey Kicks	6	10-15 Reps
Wall Mountain Climber	15	15 - 20 Reps
Wall Downward Facing Dog	31	20 Seconds

Day 16

Exercise	Number	Reps / Duration
Forearm Stretch	34	20 Seconds
Wall Lunges	7	10 Reps
Wall Touches	16	10 Reps
Move the Wall	22	20-30 Seconds
Wall Hip Thrust	8	10 - 15 Reps
Wall Scissors Kicks	18	15 - 20 Reps
Chin Tucks Against Wall	32	15 Seconds

Day 17

Exercise	Number	Reps / Duration
Wall Single Leg Balance	37	10 - 15 Seconds
Wall Kickbacks	5	10 - 15 Reps
Wall Dead Bug	19	5 - 10 Reps
Move the Wall	24	20-30 Seconds
Wall Pike Leg Extension	9	10 Reps
Wall Mountain Climber	15	15 - 20 Reps
Wall Roll Down	33	20 Seconds

Day 18

Exercise	Number	Reps / Duration
Wall Supported Single Squat	36	5 -10 Reps
Wall Hip Thrust	8	10 - 15 Reps
Wall Touches	16	10 Reps
Wall Seated Arm Pulses	25	10 - 15 Reps
Wall Calf Raises	10	10 - 15 Reps
Seated Side Bends	28	10 Reps
Wall Downward Facing Dog	31	20 Seconds

Day 19

Exercise	Number	Reps / Duration
Wall Quad Stretch	39	15 Seconds
Wall Squats Holds	1	20-30 Seconds
Wall Plank	11	20-30 Seconds
Wall Push-Ups	20	15 - 20 Reps
Wall Sidekicks	4	10 - 15 Reps
Wall Toe Touches	13	10 Reps
Wall Chest Opener	29	15 Seconds

Day 20

Exercise	Number	Reps / Duration
Plantar Fascia Stretch	38	15 Seconds
Wall Squad Sliding	2	10 Reps
Wall Side Plank	12	20-30 Seconds
Wall Arm Circles	23	5-10 Reps
Wall Kickbacks	5	10 - 15 Reps
Wall Abdominal Crunches	14	10 Reps
Wall Thoracic Elbow Extension	30	2 X 10 Seconds

Day 21

Exercise	Number	Reps / Duration
Wall Assisted Side Lunge Stretch	35	15 Seconds / Side
Wall Lateral Squad	3	10 - 15 Reps
Abdominal Twist	17	20 Reps
Diamond Wall Pushups	21	10 - 15 Reps
Wall Donkey Kicks	6	10-15 Reps
Wall Mountain Climber	15	15 - 20 Reps
Wall Downward Facing Dog	31	20 Seconds

Day 22

Exercise	Number	Reps / Duration
Forearm Stretch	34	20 Seconds
Wall Lunges	7	10 Reps
Wall Touches	16	10 Reps
Move the Wall	22	20-30 Seconds
Wall Hip Thrust	8	10 - 15 Reps
Wall Scissors Kicks	18	15 - 20 Reps
Chin Tucks Against Wall	32	15 Seconds

Day 23

Exercise	Number	Reps / Duration
Wall Single Leg Balance	37	10 - 15 Seconds
Wall Kickbacks	5	10 - 15 Reps
Wall Dead Bug	19	5 - 10 Reps
Move the Wall	24	20-30 Seconds
Wall Pike Leg Extension	9	10 Reps
Wall Mountain Climber	15	15 - 20 Reps
Wall Roll Down	33	20 Seconds

Day 24

Exercise	Number	Reps / Duration
Wall Supported Single Squat	36	5 -10 Reps
Wall Hip Thrust	8	10 - 15 Reps
Wall Touches	16	10 Reps
Wall Seated Arm Pulses	25	10 - 15 Reps
Wall Calf Raises	10	10 - 15 Reps
Seated Side Bends	28	10 Reps
Wall Downward Facing Dog	31	20 Seconds

Day 25

Exercise	Number	Reps / Duration
Wall Quad Stretch	39	15 Seconds
Wall Squats Holds	1	20-30 Seconds
Wall Plank	11	20-30 Seconds
Wall Push-Ups	20	15 - 20 Reps
Wall Sidekicks	4	10 - 15 Reps
Wall Toe Touches	13	10 Reps
Wall Chest Opener	29	15 Seconds

Day 26

Exercise	Number	Reps / Duration
Plantar Fascia Stretch	38	15 Seconds
Wall Squad Sliding	2	10 Reps
Wall Side Plank	12	20-30 Seconds
Wall Arm Circles	23	5-10 Reps
Wall Kickbacks	5	10 - 15 Reps
Wall Abdominal Crunches	14	10 Reps
Wall Thoracic Elbow Extension	30	2 X 10 Seconds

Day 27

Exercise	Number	Reps / Duration
Wall Assisted Side Lunge Stretch	35	15 Seconds / Side
Wall Lateral Squad	3	10 - 15 Reps
Abdominal Twist	17	20 Reps
Diamond Wall Pushups	21	10 - 15 Reps
Wall Donkey Kicks	6	10-15 Reps
Wall Mountain Climber	15	15 - 20 Reps
Wall Downward Facing Dog	31	20 Seconds

Day 28

Exercise	Number	Reps / Duration
Forearm Stretch	34	20 Seconds
Wall Lunges	7	10 Reps
Wall Touches	16	10 Reps
Move the Wall	22	20-30 Seconds
Wall Hip Thrust	8	10 - 15 Reps
Wall Scissors Kicks	18	15 - 20 Reps
Chin Tucks Against Wall	32	15 Seconds

Day 29

Exercise	Number	Reps / Duration
Wall Single Leg Balance	37	10 - 15 Seconds
Wall Kickbacks	5	10 - 15 Reps
Wall Dead Bug	19	5 - 10 Reps
Move the Wall	24	20-30 Seconds
Wall Pike Leg Extension	9	10 Reps
Wall Mountain Climber	15	15 - 20 Reps
Wall Roll Down	33	20 Seconds

Day 30

Exercise	Number	Reps / Duration
Wall Supported Single Squat	36	5 -10 Reps
Wall Hip Thrust	8	10 - 15 Reps
Wall Touches	16	10 Reps
Wall Side Plank with Arm Raises	25	10 - 15 Reps
Wall Calf Raises	10	10 - 15 Reps
Seated Side Bends	28	10 Reps
Wall Downward Facing Dog	31	20 Seconds

15-Minute Pilates Workouts

1. Repeat every exercise for at least "10 - 15" times or "20 - 30" seconds for a static exercise for each side of your body.

2. Make 3 - 5 rounds. You can take a short break after each round.

3. Enjoy the endorphins. :)

WORKOUT 1

1. WALL SQUATS HOLDS

25. WALL LATERAL PULLDOWN

16. WALL TOUCHES

40. "FIGURE 4" WALL HIP STRETCH

15-Minute Pilates Workouts

1. Repeat every exercise for at least "10 - 15" times or "20 - 30" seconds for a static exercise for each side of your body.

2. Make 3 - 5 rounds. You can take a short break after each round.

3. Enjoy the endorphins. :)

WORKOUT 2

5.WALL KICKBACKS

21.DIAMOND WALL PUSH-UPS

13.WALL TOE TOUCHES

33.WALL ROLL DOWN

15-Minute Pilates Workouts

1. Repeat every exercise for at least "10 - 15" times or "20 - 30" seconds for a static exercise for each side of your body.

2. Make 3 - 5 rounds. You can take a short break after each round.

3. Enjoy the endorphins. :)

WORKOUT 3

8.WALL HIP THRUSTS

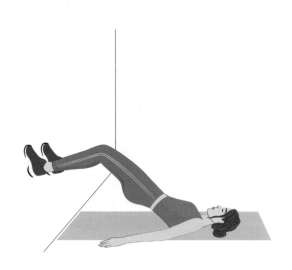

12.WALL SIDE PLANK WITH ARM RAISES

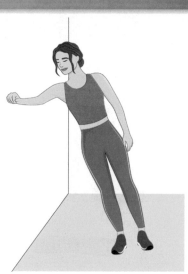

17.ABDOMINAL TWISTS

36.WALL SUPPORTED SINGLE SQUAT

15-Minute Pilates Workouts

1. Repeat every exercise for at least "10 - 15" times or "20 - 30" seconds for a static exercise for each side of your body.

2. Make 3 - 5 rounds. You can take a short break after each round.

3. Enjoy the endorphins. :)

WORKOUT 4

10. WALL CALF RAISES

20. WALL PUSH-UPS

15. WALL MOUNTAIN CLIMBERS

37. WALL SINGLE LEG BALANCE

15-Minute Pilates Workouts

1. Repeat every exercise for at least "10 - 15" times or "20 - 30" seconds for a static exercise for each side of your body.

2. Make 3 - 5 rounds. You can take a short break after each round.

3. Enjoy the endorphins. :)

WORKOUT 5

4. WALL SIDEKICKS

22. WALL TRICEPS EXTENSIONS

12. WALL SIDE PLANK

29. WALL CHEST OPENER

BONUS CHAPTER 1: CREATING LASTING HABITS

Every action you take is a vote for the type of person you wish to become.

—James Clear

To create lasting habits, you will need to apply a principle called habit stacking, a term that the author, James Clear, uses to explain how habits are formed. Habit stacking is the act of connecting your frequent behaviors to new habits. For instance, identify one behavior that you do every day without fail, and then add your new habit to that behavior. So, an individual who brushes their teeth first thing in the morning and wants to add Pilates can focus on practicing immediately after they brush their teeth.

According to Clear (n.d.), you will most likely remember to perform the new habit if it is closely linked to one of your frequent behaviors, as it will act as a cue to remind the brain to practice the new behavior. You can take the other steps listed below to continue building lasting habits.

Start With a Tiny Habit

A lot of us believe that small changes will not make a difference in our lifestyles. Lepera (2021) stated in her book that in order to create true transformation, we start small by keeping one small promise to ourselves daily. Remember this when the thought of creating a new workout routine feels overwhelming for you.

Be Consistent With Timing

Setting a time to practice your new habit will act as a cue for your brain to engage in it. For instance, if you want to practice Pilates every morning, you can try wiring your mind like this: "practice Pilates every day at 9:00 am after I brush my teeth." If you stack a new habit like so and set a time, it will more likely become automatic.

Celebrate Small Milestones

Having a large goal attached to your new habits is one way to keep you motivated. However, if you remain focused on that alone, you may become discouraged when it isn't happening quickly enough. Instead, set small rewards for yourself, which will get you excited to continue making habit changes.

For instance, if you want to become more flexible, stretching every day is a habit you have to maintain. If you want to stay motivated as you pursue flexibility, set small mileston rewards, such as getting your favorite smoothie after you have stretched consistently fo a week.

Design a Pilates Playlist

Listening to music is a technique you can use to activate different emotions in your body and enhance your mood. Designing a Pilates playlist will help motivate you to practice and get you in the mood to work out.

Schedule "Pilates Dates"

Making Pilates fun is a way to push yourself to practice often because you are most likely to pursue something that you enjoy. Setting Pilates dates and listening to a podcast or audiobook while you work out will make you excited for your next session every time, helping you get to your fitness goals quicker.

Habits are intricately woven into our brains and nervous systems, and as you change old unhealthy habits to create new ones, you may be met with emotional and mental resistance. Recognize that those are your old patterns throwing a fit and trying to keep you in a familiar pattern.

You can definitely move past this, girl! The simple act of being aware of when and where in your body you feel resistance will help you move through it successfully. Be compassionate towards yourself as you set and focus on new habits one at a time.

BONUS CHAPTER 2: NUTRITION PLAN FOR MAXIMIZING RESULTS

Your journey to achieving physical and mental transformation also requires a healthy diet. If you have been following fad diets and drinking weight-loss pills or drinks, put them aside because they do not offer benefits in the long run. If you make significant changes in the foods you eat in the long term, you will be able to maintain your fitness results, and keep excess weight off.

Good nutrition is the practice of eating a healthy and balanced diet during all your meal times. It may also mean adding necessary supplements like vitamins and minerals. Good nutrition is comprised of a healthy plate, which includes servings of vegetables, fruits, and proteins.

A well-balanced diet will help build new muscles and tissues, which will enhance your fitness results. It will also reduce your risk of getting diseases, boost your immune system, increase your energy levels, improve your mental well-being, and lower your blood pressure.

Effective Strategies to Create a Nutritional Plan That Maximizes Results

As with anything else in life, in order to achieve what we desire, we need to create strategies and systems that support our goals. The first step, just like with exercises, is to set a nutrition goal. Consider these questions: Do you want to lose weight? Do you want to drink less sodas? Do you want to eat more fruit and vegetable servings with your daily meals? The nutrition goals you have written for yourself should align with your exercise goals. If your fitness goal is to lose weight, then you should aim to eat more portions of fruit and vegetables while cutting back on processed carbs, especially three hours before you go to bed.

When you are creating a nutrition plan to support your goals, it will be helpful to think about foods that you want to add rather than those you want to exclude. Remember, your body and life go in the direction of your mind. Thus, if you keep thinking about what foods you are removing from your diet, then you will eventually fill your body with unhealthy foods that will not help you meet your goals.

Aside from setting your goals, it is important to know your body type and eat according to it. If you have a higher percentage of fat in your body, then having a nutrition plan with low-carb meals will ensure you maintain a healthy weight and avoid obesity. If you tend to be on the slimmer side and have a low body fat percentage, eat more starchy foods to make sure that you have enough energy stored in your body to carry out your daily activities. Planning your meals and creating a meal schedule will help you be consistent. Try meal prepping and shopping at whole food stores. A little tip when you go grocery shopping next time is to eat before you go shopping to avoid buying foods that you do not need. You can also make a mental map of which aisles in the store have the healthy foods that you need to avoid looking at foods that you will not need.

Macronutrients

Macronutrients are nutrients that the body needs in large doses. They are required in larger quantities by the body because they are the body's main source of energy. These macronutrients come from carbohydrates, proteins, and fats. According to Mae (2021), we need to consume 45–65% carbohydrates, 20–35% fats, and 10–35% protein in order to provide the body with essential nutrition.

Micronutrients

Micronutrients are nutrients that the body needs in smaller doses, and any excess is excreted from the kidneys as waste. Although carbohydrates are the main source of energy, vitamins and minerals also help produce energy and reduce the risk of diseases.

Weight Loss Tips

Although health standards recommend a certain amount of macronutrients for individuals to take, the quantity also depends on the individual's fitness goals and current weight. Various cultural backgrounds also influence how much you consume. Therefore, it is necessary for you to seek professional assistance to know your body mass index and fat percentage to determine how much you should be eating

When you are on a weight-loss diet, you will need to stay away from carbohydrates that come from refined foods, such as muffins, cakes, and white breads. Healthy carbohydrates that you can add to your diet on your weight-loss journey include brown rice, sweet potatoes, oats, and pumpkins.

BONUS CHAPTER 3: BIOHACK YOUR BODY

Biohacking is a steady process of using various tricks to enhance your body's ability to perform. You can use biohacking techniques such as the ones below to enhance your physical, mental, and emotional health. When you consistently perform these techniques, you will see an improvement in the quality of your life and reach your fitness goals quicker.

Daily Walking

Walking helps reduce stress in your body. Mood enhancers–endorphins–are released when you walk, which helps clear your mind. Apart from that, walking supports heart function and improves blood circulation throughout your body. Walking is accessible to everyone because it is a low-impact exercise. The more steps you take, the better it is for your overall health because consistently engaging your cardiovascular system helps promote healthier and longer life.

Walking is also a good exercise to help you lose weight and maintain that weight loss. One study by Ouerghi et al. (2021) found that acute exercises like walking suppress the production of ghrelin–the hunger hormone found in the stomach–while longer and more energetic exercises like running increase its production. Aim to take 7,000 steps per day (a benchmark associated with increased longevity) or 10,000 for more cardiovascular activity, even if you do not engage in any other physical activity.

Jumping

Rigorous activities like jumping can help increase bone density, build muscle tone, enhance metabolism, boost heart health, and regulate your mood. Two to three minutes of jumping activities in the morning can activate your lymphatic system, which helps your body expel toxic wastes, enhancing your immunity, health, and vitality. Some examples of jumping workouts you can do are trampoline exercises, jumping jacks, skipping, jogging on the spot, jump squats, and lateral jumps.

Sun Exposure

Sunlight has many benefits for the human body, including enhanced sleep. The sun's rays boost the production of vitamin D in your body, which helps reduce symptoms of depression and manage weight.

The rays from the sun also aid in the regulation of your circadian rhythms and synchronization of your body's internal clock for better sleep. It is advised to soak in the morning sun before it becomes too hot. To absorb more sunlight, sit outside without glasses or lenses when the sun is rising as part of your morning routine.

Red and Infrared Light Therapy: Dual Photo Biomodulation for Cellular Healing

Red light and infrared light emit rays that help heal the human body on a cellular level. Red light has waves that range from 620 to 700 nanometers, while infrared light waves range from 800 to 1,000 nanometers. Both of these lights increase the synthesis of adenosine triphosphate (ATP) which improves the functional ability of the mitochondria in the cells.

As the cells are stimulated, collagen production and cell turnover rate increase, reducing signs of aging while improving skin conditions by healing wounds. These light waves penetrate the skin and cause biological reactions that improve blood circulation, decrease tissue inflammation, and hasten tissue healing. This biohack provides a revitalizing, non-invasive method to improve general well-being and cellular health.

Cold Exposure

Cold exposure is the practice of immersing oneself in temperatures below 15 degrees Celsius or 59 degrees Fahrenheit. Cold exposure helps with weight loss because it activates brown fats in the body, which are known to help your body burn calories and regulate fat metabolism and sugar levels.

The benefits of cold exposure also include improving the cardiovascular, immune, and endocrine systems. Swimming, immersing, or bathing in cold water also has mental health benefits and can make you more focused as you go about your day. Your hormones cycles and circadian rhythms are also more likely to be balanced. Your ability to face environmental stressors will increase due to stimulated adrenaline.

Cold exposure can also help tighten the pelvic region and give you glowing skin. You can start with showering in cold water and then later seek a trained professional to try full-body immersion dips in colder waters. Another way to immerse yourself in lower temperatures is to engage in physical activities, such as running or swimming in the cold weather.

EMF Management – Melatonin Secretion Enhancement

Blue light negatively affects the retina in the eyes, which can cause eye strain and phototoxicity. It is advised to take breaks from screens, especially before going to bed, as it will interfere with your sleep cycle and affect your body clock. Poor sleep hygiene will affect your energy levels and ability to carry out day-to-day tasks. Minimizing this exposure to blue light and artificial light helps the body secrete melatonin, which is an antioxidant in the body.

Increased melatonin levels also help the cells repair themselves and protect the body from oxidative stress. Turn off EMFs and Wi-Fi routers during the night and put your phone on airplane mode. If you wish to use your phone in the evening, consider wearing blue light-blocking glasses so that you can optimize your sleep.

Autophagy

Autophagy is a process where the cells in the body eliminate toxic substances, promoting cellular health and longevity. Considering that this process occurs at night, you can help facilitate it by abstaining from food two to three hours before bed.

Salt and Lime Water

Our bodies need electrolytes to function well. The muscles and nerves need a good balance of electrolytes like sodium, calcium, and magnesium to enhance our body's performance.

Adding salt to your water is an effective way to replenish electrolytes in your body as well as maintain the right balance of electrolytes. Aim to use filtered water when possible and ensure that the water is warm because warm salt water is therapeutic and can help with digestion.

Drink salt water in moderation because too much salt in the body can cause kidney failure. High-quality salts like Himalayan salt and sea salts like Celtic sea salt are known to work better for enhancing electrolytes in the body, so grab a hold of them whenever you can. For added taste, more electrolytes, and digestive help, squeeze in some lime juice.

Sauna

Saunas can eliminate from the body the presence of alcohol, nicotine, and heavy metal deposits, which may be carcinogenic. These toxins are expelled through perspiration caused by the heat in the sauna, detoxifying both the skin and the body. Saunas can also be used to treat acne and other skin conditions, improve blood circulation, and enhance weight loss. Integrate saunas as part of your routine whenever you can.

Micronutrient Supplementation

Due to today's fast-paced modern lifestyle, a modern diet of quick eating and fast foods has risen. This diet has nutritional gaps and does not nourish your body with what it needs. Not only that, but the poor quality of the soil where crops grow has led to micronutrient deficiencies in our foods.

To fill these nutritional gaps, consume active forms of micronutrients. For instance, instead of taking folic acid, take it in its active form, folate, which will improve energy production in the body and enhance your body's immunity. Taking active micronutrients will also help the body's ability to absorb other nutrients and utilize them. Personally, rely on supplements from the brand *NOW*, with which I am not affiliated in any way.

Biohacking is a good addition to your fitness routine because of its long-term benefits when practiced consistently. These biohacking methods often do not cost much and are generally safe. You do not have to practice all the techniques all at once. Do only what feels good for your body, and if you just want to stick with wall Pilates for now, that's totally okay.

CONCLUSION

Physical transformation is a challenging yet beautiful journey because it gives you more than just a better body. You will feel more confident, grounded, and clear-headed. Pursuing physical fitness goals can also help you build your emotional resilience as you push yourself past old unhealthy habits to create new ones and endure strength-training Pilates sessions.

Pursuing wall Pilates will be an exciting start to better things ahead for you; just trust the process as you pace yourself. Be gentle with your body and compassionate to your soul while you do your best to transform it. Reading this book until the end is already a sign that you are ready for what is to come, and we are excited for you as you set out on this fitness journey.

HELP ME SPREAD THE WORD

I hope you have been able to extract all the wisdom and knowledge from this book and put the challenges into action. Please don't forget to leave a review on Amazon, and let me know how this book has helped you. I would love to hear the transformation results that you have achieved after putting the content of this book into practice.

As a new author your reviews will serve as inspiration for me to create better material and motivate me to keep coming up with highly informative books that will help you achieve your goals.

It has been a pleasure to be your guide on your fitness journey. Continue striving for better health; I am rooting for you!

Alex Harper

REFERENCES

1. Allarakha, S. (2020). *What are the benefits of jumping?* MedicineNet. https://www.medicinenet.com/what_are_the_benefits_ of_jumping/article.htm

2. Alloz, T. (2020). Oatmeal with fresh berry fruits in a bowl [Online Image]. In *Pexels*. https://www.pexels.com/photo/oatmeal-with-fresh-berry-fruits-in-a-bowl-5604832/

3. Alonso, M. (2021). Fit Asian woman doing supine spinal twist on yoga mat [Online Image]. In *Pexels*. https://www.pexels.com/photo/fit-asian-woman-doing-supine-spinal-twist-on-yoga-mat-7592444/

4. American Council on Exercise. (2022). *Pilates: Health benefits, how to get started, and how to get better (everyday health).* Ace Fitness. https://www.acefitness.org/about-ace/press-room/in-the-news/8174/pilates-health-benefits-how-to-get-started-and-how-to-get-better-everyday-health/

5. Barnes, M. (2023, November 13). *What exactly is wall pilates? Plus 5 wall pilates exercises to try at home.* YouAligned™. https://youaligned.com/fitness/what-is-wall-pilates/

6. Centers for Disease Control and Prevention. (2022, April 27). *Benefits of physical activity.* Centers for Disease Control and Prevention; CDC. https://www.cdc.gov/physicalactivity/basics/pa-health/index.htm#:~:text=Regular%20physical%20activity%20is%20one

7. Claire, R. (2020). Person holding piece of fried chicken above plate with food [Online Image]. In *Pexels*. https://www.pexels.com/photo/person-holding-piece-of-fried-chicken-above-plate-with-food-5531301/

8. Clear, J. (n.d.). *Habit stacking: How to build new habits by taking advantage of old ones.* James Clear. https://jamesclear.com/habit-stacking

9. Costa, F. (2023). Woman in sportswear jumping rope on a running track [Online Image]. In *Pexels*. https://www.pexels.com/photo/woman-in-sportswear-jumping-rope-on-a-running-track-19198882/

10. Cottonbro Studio. (2020). Person listening to music on a smartphone [Online Image]. In *Pexels*. https://www.pexels.com/photo/person-listening-to-music-on-a-smartphone-5077396/

11. Dato-on, A. (2021). Jumping woman in sportswear [Online Image]. In *Pexels*. https://www.pexels.com/photo/jumping-woman-in-sportswear-9645064/

12. Frame Fitness. (2022, June 22). *How the pilates mind-body connection works for you.* Frame Fitness. https://www.framefitness.com/blog/news/how-the-pilates-mind-body-connection-works-for-you

13. Grabowska, K. (2020). Thoughtful young woman holding mat in hands [Online Image]. In *Pexels*. https://www.pexels.com/photo/thoughtful-young-woman-holding-mat-in-hands-4498511/

14. Gupta, A. (2023, October 26). *7 reasons why you should drink warm salt water everyday.* Health Shots. https://www.healthshots.com/healthy-eating/nutrition/benefits-of-warm-salt-water/

15. Horne, B. (2023, May 9). *Pilates and weight loss* (D. Hildreth, Ed.). Medical News Today. https://www.medicalnewstoday.com/articles/is-pilates-good-for-weight-loss

16. Hyatt, M. (2022, March 7). *4 steps to create a new habit.* Full Focus. https://fullfocus.co/4-steps-to-create-a-new-habit/

17. Kamornboonyarush, A. (2018). Photo of person holding alarm clock [Online Image]. In *Pexels*. https://www.pexels.com/photo/photo-of-person-holding-alarm-clock-1028741/

18. Kelly, G. (2022, July 5). *Are blue light glasses effective?* Mayo Clinic Health System. https://www.cdc.gov/physicalactivity/basics/pahealth/index.htm#:~:text=Regular%20physical%20activity%20is%20one

19. Kilinski, F. (2023, April 25). *Walking for brain power.* LinkedIn. https://www.linkedin.com/pulse/walking-brain-power-fran-kilinski/

20. Koolshooters. (2020). Photograph of a woman doing yoga in her living room [Online Image]. In *Pexels*. https://www.pexels.

com/photo/photograph-of-a-woman-doing-yoga-in-her-living-room-6246251/

21. Lepera, N. (2021). *How to do the work* (1st ed.). HarperCollins Publishing. (Original work published 2021)

22. M, S. (2021). *What is good nutrition and a healthy diet?* Medicine Net. https://www.medicinenet.com/what_is_good_nutrition_and_a_healthy_diet/article.htm

23. Mae, A. (2021, September 30). *Macronutrients: Definition, importance, and food sources.* Medical News Today. https://www.medicalnewstoday.com/articles/what-are-macronutrients

24. Mazzo, L. (2024, January 8). *Wall pilates is predicted to be 2024's biggest fitness trend—worth a try?* POPSUGAR Fitness UK. https://www.popsugar.co.uk/fitness/wall-pilates-workout-49329079

25. Mind 2 Body. (2017, January 25). *Inspirational pilates quotes.* Mind 2 Body™ Pilates Studio. https://www.mind2body.net/blog-content/2017/1/25/pilates-quotes#:~:text=Pilates%20Quotes%20by%20Joseph%20Pilates

26. Mukhwana, J. (2022, November 9). *20 wall pilates benefits: You'll wish you knew about these sooner!* BetterMe Blog. https://betterme.world/articles/wall-pilates-benefits/#3_Improved_Spinal_Alignment

27. Munuhe, N. (2023, May 10). *What is wall pilates? A guide for the beginner.* BetterMe Blog. https://betterme.world/articles/what-is-wall-pilates/

28. Neumann, K. D. (2023, August 17). *What is biohacking and how does it work?* Forbes Health. https://www.forbes.com/health/wellness/biohacking/

29. Ogle, M. (2020, December 11). *How to find your neutral spine position.* Verywell Fit. https://www.verywellfit.com/how-to-find-neutral-spine-position-2704586

30. Ouerghi, N., Feki, M., Bragazzi, N. L., Knechtle, B., Hill, L., Nikolaidis, P. T., & Bouassida, A. (2021). Ghrelin response to acute and chronic exercise: Insights and implications from a systematic review of the literature. *Sports Medicine, 51*(11), 2389–2410. https://doi.org/10.1007/s40279-021-01518-6

31. Pilates Reformers. (2023, August 9). *Pilates and breathwork: Harnessing the power of breath for enhanced focus and energy.* Pilates Reformers Plus. https://pilatesreformersplus.com/blogs/news/pilates-and-breathwork-harnessing-the-power-of-breath-for-enhanced-focus-and-energy#:~:text=By%20breathing%20deeply%20into%20your

32. Pilates, K. (2018, January 6). *Am I improving? Body awareness and the mind-body connection in pilates.* Kinetic Pilates Site. https://www.kineticpilates.com/post/am-i-improving-body-awareness-and-the-mind-body-connection-in-pilates#:~:text=Pilates%20improves%20the%20relationship%20between%20your%20mind%20and%20body&text=Concentration%20is%20one%20of%20the

33. Pirie, K. (2020, November 25). *What is the endomorph diet? Health experts explain everything you need to know.* Good Housekeeping. https://www.goodhousekeeping.com/health/diet-nutrition/a34744438/what-is-endomorph-diet/

34. Quin, E., Rafferty, S., & Tomlinson, C. (2015). Principles and components of cooling down. In *Safe Dance Practice.* Human Kinetics. https://us.humankinetics.com/blogs/excerpt/principles-and-components-of-cooling-down

35. RDNE Stock Project. (2021a). Woman doing yoga in a gym [Online Image]. In *Pexels.* https://www.pexels.com/photo/woman-doing-yoga-in-a-gym-6539859/

36. RTR Pilates. (2023, December 5). *Why pilates is the ultimate confidence booster.* RTR Pilates. https://rtrpilates.com/pilate and-self-esteem/#:~:text=Pilates%20helps%20us%20to%20become

37. Skye, E. (n.d.). *Why repetition is so important for your results.* Emilyskyefit.com. https://emilyskyefit.com/blog/show/1006 why-repetition-is-so-important-for-your-results

38. Wetton, D. (2019). Yoga images and pictures [Online Image]. In *Unsplash.* https://unsplash.com/photos/woman-performin yoga-t1NEMSm1rgI

39. World Rugby Passport. (n.d.). *World rugby passport - principles and guidelines for an effective warm-up.* World Rugby Passpo Retrieved January 25, 2024, from https://passport.world.rugby/conditioning-for-rugby/introduction-to-conditionir children/warm-up-cool-down-and-flexibility/principles-and-guidelines-for-an-effective-warm-up/

Made in the USA
Columbia, SC
21 April 2024

34681109R00050